ROB WESTON'S
GUIDE TO
METHOD ACTING

for **Prestigious Talented Performers**

with **Ambitious Goals**

for **Career Advancement**

ROB WESTON

Rob Weston's Guide To Method Acting For Prestigious Talented Performers With Ambitious Goals For Career Advancement. Copyright 2019 Rob Weston. All rights reserved.

Printed in the United States of America. No part of this book may be used or reproduced in any manner without prior written consent except in the case of brief quotations embodied in critical articles and reviews.

Cover design by: Alejandra Weston.

Queries to: **contact@moviestarrating.com**

ISBN: 978-1-7341683-0-3

DISCLAIMER

This book is not meant as a guide, self-help program or educational program. It is designed and presented solely for entertainment purposes only. You should always seek the services of a competent professional before beginning any improvement program (personal, professional or otherwise). The author and publisher are under no circumstances offering this book (and the contents herein) as any type of psychological, legal, educational, financial or any other kind of professional or career advice or improvement whatsoever, nor as any kind of personal advice, including but not limited to growth or personal development. While best efforts have been used in preparing this book, the author and publisher make no representations, warranties or guarantees of any kind and assume no liabilities of any kind with respect to the accuracy or completeness of the contents of this book and specifically disclaim any implied warranties of merchantability or fitness of use for a particular purpose. Neither the publisher nor author shall be held liable or responsible to any person or entity with respect to (and without limitation) any loss or incidental loss or consequential damages caused, or alleged to have been caused, directly or indirectly, by the information contained herein or any physical, psychological, emotional, financial, legal or commercial damages, including, but not limited to, special, incidental, consequential or other damages. Our views and rights are the same: You are responsible for your own choices, actions, and results. **This is a work of fiction.** Any references to real events including but not limited to, agents, attorneys, directors, producers or places are used fictitiously. The story, incidents, characters and entities contained herein are fictional. Any likeness to actual persons, either living or dead, events or places are strictly coincidental.

JUST IN CASE YOU DIDN'T READ THE
DISCLAIMER...

THIS BOOK IS DESIGNED AND PRESENTED SOLELY FOR ENTERTAINMENT PURPOSES.

*This book does **NOT** follow the rules...
It does **NOT** adhere to standard logic
or conventional numbering either. Why?
Because beginners learn the rules...*
Masters own them.

CONTENTS

*	FOREWORD	1
**	INTRODUCTION	3

CHAPTER 11 - "THE POWER OF YOUR VOICE"

STEP 11	"THE MIRROR"	7
STEP 16	"FORGET WHAT THEY SAY"	8
STEP 19	"REACH FOR THE STARS"	9-10

CHAPTER 22 - "YADA… YADA..."

STEP 29	"THE BLAME GAME"	15-16
STEP 37	"THE DIAL TONE..."	17-18
STEP 65	"LET IT SHINE"	19-20

CHAPTER 37 - "ENLISTING AN AGENT"

STEP 77	"DRESSING THE PART"	25-26
STEP 88	"THE CASTING COUCH"	27-28
STEP 89	"THE PRICE OF DIGNITY"	29-30
STEP 98	"MAKE IT BIG!"	31-32

CHAPTER 49 - "NOTHING BUT CRICKETS"

STEP 105	"NO REGRETS"	37-38

CONTENTS

STEP 112	"PATIENCE BLOWS"	39
STEP 126	"NO SURRENDER!"	40-41
STEP 136	"PATIENCE PAYS!"	42

CHAPTER 69 - "DOMINATING THE FRAME"

STEP 170	"NOW YOU SEE ME…"	47-48
STEP 171	"THE HUMAN FOUNTAIN"	49-50
STEP 176	"THE ENEMY"	51-52

CHAPTER 79 - "PREP PREP PREP"

STEP 189	"LASER FOCUSED"	57-58
STEP 196	"HELLO AGAIN, OLD FRIEND!"	59
STEP 201	"WHERE DO I LIVE?"	60-61-62

CHAPTER 83 - "DARKNESS OF REJECTION"

STEP 210	"FAILURE DOES NOT EXIST"	67-68
STEP 229	"GRASS ISN'T GREENER"	69-70
STEP 233	"SAME SH*T DIFFERENT DAY…"	71

CHAPTER 94 - "A FALSE DAWN?"

| STEP 254 | "WHERE'S MY LIFE JACKET?" | 75-76 |

CONTENTS

| STEP 261 | "OUT WITH THE OLD" | 77-78 |
| STEP 274 | "SAY MY NAME!" | 79-80 |

CHAPTER 109 - "GOOD THINGS COME TO THOSE WHO..."

STEP 280	"VICTORY!"	85-86
STEP 284	"FRONT END OR BACK END"	87-88
STEP 290	"EMERGENCY FACE TIME"	89-90
STEP 293	"LAW UNTO THEMSELVES"	91-92

CHAPTER 120 - "THE NEW YOU!"

STEP 294	"DO I GET A CAPE?"	97-98
STEP 297	"EMBRACE THE MISTAKES"	99-100
STEP 299	"PLAYING DETECTIVE"	101-102

CHAPTER 144 - "WORLD FAMOUS!"

STEP 300	"NO LIMITS"	107-108
STEP 311	"FIESTA FOREVER"	109-110
STEP 325	"I'D LIKE TO THANK..."	111-112

CHAPTER 155 - "CROSSROADS"

| STEP 333 | "GROWING STALE?" | 117-118 |

CONTENTS

STEP 337   "ANOTHER SIDE OF YOU!"   119-120

STEP 356   "IT'S NOT OVERNIGHT"   121-122

CHAPTER 169 - "PASSING ON THE MESSAGE"

STEP 377   "THE FINAL STEP"   127-128

"METHOD IS A WAY OF LIFE"

Rob Weston

FOREWORD

This book was created for all the performers in this world... but if you are **NOT** a performer (and let's face it, we all are) **don't stress**. As if you read this book carefully you will find the secrets within are for you too. But first a **WARNING** of the highest regard...

ONCE YOU READ THIS BOOK YOU CANNOT UNREAD IT.

THE CONTENTS OF THIS BOOK ARE VERY POWERFUL.

THIS BOOK IS NOT MEANT FOR JUST ANYONE. IT IS ONLY FOR THOSE WHO TRULY WISH TO TRIUMPH IN LIFE.

Each step touches the inner soul in a way never achieved before. Such power needs to be absorbed slowly and channeled into the inner psyche.

Read just one step a day, otherwise, the risk of overdosing on the wisdom herein could well become a reality.

Some of the steps may sound like the utterings of some mad gibberish, but study them closely, read them over and over, ingest them slowly and you too will understand them for what they are.

So go forth my friend. Read on. Follow this guide and you too can unlock the true possibilities of **YOU!**

INTRODUCTION

There are four personality types, which one are **YOU?**

1 - Intelligent and committed (Ideal!).

2 - Intelligent and workshy (a shame!).

3 - Stupid and committed (a problem!).

4 - Stupid and workshy (<u>OH SH*T!</u>).

If you're a "1" or "2", read on!

If you're a "3" or "4", why the hell are you even reading this book???

CHAPTER 11

"THE POWER OF YOUR VOICE"

CHAPTER 11

STEP 11

"THE MIRROR"

When you look in the mirror what do you see? I'll tell you what you see...

You see **YESTERDAY!**

Perhaps you're a stoner, who lives life on the sofa?

Maybe you just can't piss straight even if your life depended on it?

IT DOESN'T MATTER WHAT YOU SEE.

As with this book all that is about to **CHANGE.** Repeat after me.

Every dog has its day... And today it's this dog's day!

Every dog has its day... And today it's this dog's day!!

EVERY DOG HAS ITS DAY... AND TODAY IT'S THIS DOG'S DAY!!!

"THE POWER OF YOUR VOICE"

STEP 16

"FORGET WHAT THEY SAY"

Everyone tells you to **"just be yourself"** right?

WELL, THAT'S FINE IF YOU KNOW WHO THE HELL YOU ARE!

And even if you know who the hell you are, chances are you're probably not the person you think you are anyway... or even the person you want to be.

So let's cut to the chase.

You, yes **YOU**, can be **ANYONE** or **ANYTHING** you want to be...

Well almost... You can't be POTUS or FLOTUS or the Pope...

OR MAYBE YOU CAN?

So close your eyes...

Focus.

And let these words sink in...

I WILL BE ANYONE OR ANYTHING I WANT TO BE.

CHAPTER 11

STEP 19

"REACH FOR THE STARS"

THE QUESTION IS WHO EXACTLY DO YOU WANT TO BE?

This is just as relevant to **you, the person,** as it to **you the performer**.

If your dream is to strike it big by becoming the lead actor in a toe fungus commercial then you my friend, are reading the wrong book.

Please note. This book is not for a**holes.

This book is about **DISCOVERING** your inner **GREATNESS.**

So dream higher!

Reach for the stars!

Touch those **FUTURE AWARDS!**

Close your eyes... And repeat after me:

I THINK BIG!... I DREAM BIG!!... I ACT BIG!!!... I AM BIG!!!!

"THE POWER OF YOUR VOICE"

Say it **LOUDER!**...

Repeat this every morning!!

Do it **EVERY DAY** until you shout it from the rooftops, or wherever the hell you are.

Note. I do NOT, however, recommend doing this in a public restroom.

These words are your **MANTRA.**

NEVER EVER FORGET THEM!

Right now you're a caterpillar.

Soon, with this book, you will become a chrysalis.

Put the work in now and you will become a butterfly!

CHAPTER 22

"YADA… YADA..."

CHAPTER 22

STEP 29
"THE BLAME GAME"

Chances are you're reading this book because you wish to advance your career as a performer...

That, or you need some company squeezing one out on the John.

Whatever the reason, it begs the question... **why** are you not where you want to be in your career today?

Perhaps you don't know the right people?

Maybe you're not in the right circles?

All the other a**bandits in town keep getting the gigs right?

NEWSFLASH: The only person who controls your destiny is YOU.

Ask yourself: *Would the person I want to be, make excuses like that?*

HELL NO!

Excuses are for the **weak!**...

"YADA... YADA..."

Excuses are for the **phonies!...**

Excuses are for the **never do wells!...**

And with this book my friend, that is no longer you.

So it's time to **stop crying.**

It's time to stop feeling sorry for yourself.

<u>IT'S TIME TO TAKE CONTROL OF YOUR DESTINY!</u>

CHAPTER 22

STEP 37

"THE DIAL TONE..."

Today is the day...

Not tomorrow...

Or next week...

Or next month...

TODAY!

So pick up the phone and make those calls.

I know it isn't easy...

Don't worry.

Over time it will be.

Time builds ROUTINE...

Routine builds CONFIDENCE.

Eventually, this world will hear you **ROAR!**

Today is the **beginning** of the **rest of your life.**

Today is the **beginning** of your **reinvention.**

"YADA... YADA..."

TODAY IS THE BEGINNING OF THE FUTURE YOU.

No longer will you let the b*stards hold you down!

No longer will you let your insecurities dictate your future.

No longer... No longer!

CHAPTER 22

STEP 65

"LET IT SHINE"

Should I change my name?

Should you heck!!!!

YOUR NAME IS YOUR IDENTITY!

It's something you **MUST** own.

It **DOESN'T MATTER** if no one can even pronounce it...

Or if it's associated with the current laughing stock of the entire universe...

Your name is **YOU!**

SO SAY IT WITH PRIDE!

WEAR IT like an athlete proudly adorns their precious Gold Medal.

HEAR IT being screamed from the rafters by your adoring fans.

BELIEVE IN IT!

"YADA... YADA..."

YOUR NAME is the **CROWN** on top of your head.

LOVE IT AND IT WILL **SHINE** BRIGHTER THAN YOU COULD EVER IMAGINE.

CHAPTER 37

"ENLISTING AN AGENT"

CHAPTER 37

STEP 77
"DRESSING THE PART"

Got yourself an appointment with a prospective new agent? Sounds like your **'TODAY'** paid off.

But before you do anything else...

STOP!

Take a beat.

We need to take a look inside your closet...

No not the secret stash at the back!... Your clothes dummy!

Do you think that second-hand car salesman look is going to impress anyone?

And... No, your mother doesn't count!

Or that slacker surfer look you perfected back in your twenties...

DO YOU WANT TO LOOK LIKE AN UTTER A**HOLE!?

They're not a good look. They never were. Whoever the hell told you they were is not your friend. That so-

"ENLISTING AN AGENT"

called friend is an enabler. **This book speaks the truth.**

You want to impress right? So start acting like it.

Now is the time to speculate to accumulate. Starting with buying some new threads that actually f*cking fit you!

DRESS THE PART AND BECOME THE PERSON YOU WANT TO BE.

Your clothes will become your armor...

IMPENETRABLE!...

BULLETPROOF!!...

READY FOR WAR!!!

CHAPTER 37

STEP 88

"THE CASTING COUCH"

So you made it to your appointment with the agent on time?

Sitting in the waiting room?

Rocking your new threads?

Bravo!

But now my friend, you are about to enter the **lion's den**.

Through that door is the **gatekeeper to your future...**

YOUR PROSPECTIVE NEW AGENT!...

And no, I have zero idea why he has that strange red light flickering above his door...

It's okay. It's natural to feel nervous at a time like this.

Just relax.

Breathe...

Inhale...

Exhale...

"ENLISTING AN AGENT"

Feeling better right?

Good...

Because before you meet the agent who could help change your entire life, you really should ask yourself one question...

ARE YOU PREPARED TO TAKE ONE IN THAT PLACE WHERE THE SUN DON'T SHINE FOR THE SAKE OF YOUR PRECIOUS CAREER?...

WHICH, BY THE WAY, YOU DON'T EVEN HAVE YET!

CHAPTER 37

STEP 89

"THE PRICE OF DIGNITY"

You panicked and fled to the nearest restroom, didn't you?

Now you're holed up in one of the cubicles!

Note. If you're even contemplating the answer to the question posed in Step 88, then shut this book and never read another page...

This is your freaking dignity we're talking about!

IT'S YOU'RE A** GODAMMIT!!

The only thing you should stick up an a**, is your head when you're immersing yourself in the character you want to be!

Jeez... surely you can't still be having doubts about this??

Ask yourself...

What would the person I want to be, do here?

"ENLISTING AN AGENT"

They'd protect their a**, that's what they'd do!

ALWAYS PROTECT YOU'RE A**!!

AND ALWAYS… I REPEAT ALWAYS CONSULT THE PERSON YOU WANT TO BE ON YOUR FUTURE DECISIONS.

CHAPTER 37

STEP 98

"MAKE IT BIG!"

Someone once said; "If you're going to make an animal, **make a goddamn ELEPHANT**, not a freaking mouse!"

Translation: ALWAYS make a big impression!!

So *finally* you're sitting across from your prospective new agent...

Maybe he recognizes you from that thing that got canceled, on that channel no one watches.

Perhaps he's just staring at that bead of sweat slowly sliding down your forehead.

Or just maybe he doesn't have the faintest clue who the hell you even are.

After all, he's seeing twenty-five others just like you today...

Wannabes...

Has-beens...

Typecasts...

To him, you are just another number.

"ENLISTING AN AGENT"

Did I dent your ego?

Sorry, but this really isn't the time to candy coat things.

<u>TODAY IS THE NEW YOU. YOU ARE NO LONGER THE PERSON YOU WERE YESTERDAY.</u>

So shake that agent by the hand like a **champion**, with your iron grip...

Flop those brand new leather cowboy boots up on that agent's desk, like a **gunslinger** from the old west...

Smile and nod when you **disagree** with absolutely anything that agent says... Like *"Take your f*cking boots, off my f*cking desk!"*

CHAPTER 49

"NOTHING BUT CRICKETS"

CHAPTER 49

STEP 105

"NO REGRETS"

Some folks call it buyer's remorse. Right now, you my friend, are going through seller's remorse...

Did I just screw up big time with that agent?

I knew I shouldn't have roared in his face like a lion when I left!

Yep - probably was a little too much.

"Don't call us, we'll call you" ringing in your ears?

Should I call the agent or not?

Should I call a friend to ask if I should call the agent or not?

STOP...

GET A GRIP!

LIE DOWN!

DO IT NOW!

It doesn't matter where you are...

A sidewalk... A shopping mall... A bar mitzvah.

Just do it now!

Lie on that floor. Wherever you are.

Close your eyes...

Breathe...

LET YOUR IMAGINATION OVERRIDE YOUR LOGIC.

Inhale...

Exhale...

That's it...

Relax.

No one can disturb you now. You are in your place of **Zen**.

You are an **ELEPHANT**... in the forest... roaming the lands.

Your doubts are natural...

You are **GROWING**...

TRANSFORMING.

YOU WILL BE ANYONE OR ANYTHING YOU WANT TO BE.

CHAPTER 49

STEP 112
"PATIENCE BLOWS"

Still in a holding pattern?

Welcome to f*cking **purgatory!**

I know. Sucks right?

Will the agent call you and save your a**? Or not call and send you straight to hell?

You're feeling torn.

The new you wouldn't stand for this right?

I know what you're thinking...

I should go down there, bust down that agent's door and--

--WRONG!

Newsflash: That agent experienced your new powers. Imagine if you were him? Give him time.

You are in the infancy of your transformation.

That agent will remember you trust me...

YOU... ARE UNFORGETTABLE!

"NOTHING BUT CRICKETS"

STEP 126

"NO SURRENDER!"

Still nothing from that agent?!

Now is the time to METHOD this.

Remember who **YOU** are.

Remember the **POWER OF YOUR VOICE.**

Remember your **NAME.**

The new you is at peace with this silence. Hell, you laugh in the face of silence!

YOU are a PATIENCE WARRIOR...

UNFLAPPABLE.

UNFAZEABLE.

UNBREAKABLE.

Take your mind off what you can't control...

And no, that doesn't mean spending your time in the shower playing with yourself!

CHAPTER 49

BREATHE.

INHALE...

EXHALE...

Be calm.

You've got this.

Just like Step 37 said, pick up that phone and start making those calls.

A COWBOY ALWAYS GETS BACK IN THE SADDLE.

The new you cannot give in.

YOU will NEVER give in!

STEP 136

"PATIENCE PAYS!"

Well, what do you know!... That agent came through!

I told you he wouldn't be able to forget you, didn't I.

HAVE FAITH IN THE METHOD.

You my friend, are now a signed actor!

YESTERDAY'S YOU, IS THANKING TODAY'S YOU.

This is a moment to take stock and rejoice.

Return to Step 11, return to the mirror...

Every dog has its day... And today it's this dog's day!!!

Look at yourself in that mirror.

Truly look at yourself...

You did this.

You my friend, are a **hero!**

YOU ARE YOUR HERO!!

CHAPTER 69

"DOMINATING THE FRAME"

CHAPTER 69

STEP 170

"NOW YOU SEE ME..."

Your new agent wants some new headshots.

That means it's time to show your true **method range!**

But remember <u>YOU are no longer like the others</u>.

You don't follow the rules.

Hell, you only learn the rules so you can **break them!**

You are different...

SPECIAL!

Your headshots won't be black and white vanity poses.

Or selfie duck faces.

They will be your own personal trailer moments for the actor that you are...

"DOMINATING THE FRAME"

ICONIC, captured moments in **HISTORY**, of a **FUTURE SUPERHERO!**

BUT EVEN SUPERHERO'S NEED TO SHOW RANGE...

And to **SHOW** your range...

<u>YOU FIRST NEED TO LEARN THE ILLUSION... BEFORE YOU CAN BECOME THE ILLUSION!</u>

CHAPTER 69

STEP 171

"THE HUMAN FOUNTAIN"

DO NOT UNDERESTIMATE THE POWER OF A GREAT HEADSHOT.

Now is the time to bring it all!

And no, I'm not talking about ponying up what little cash you do have to hire that dodgy wardrobe stylist you met at that thing out in the desert.

I'm talking about owning your character method style!

First up, you'll need to show **EMOTION.**

Remember Step 29 when I told you to stop crying?...

Well now you've graduated to Step 171, it's time to let all those tears you've been holding inside flow...

So go ahead, cry like a baby as all the great actors can do!...

It's not easy hey?

Reach deep inside...

DEEPER!

"DOMINATING THE FRAME"

RE-DISCOVER THAT INNER TRAUMA!!...

Channel it and you too can become a human fountain.

And if all else fails, poke yourself in the eyeballs!

CHAPTER 69

STEP 176

"THE ENEMY"

So you mastered the art of crying like a baby?

I knew you would... **YOU** can do anything!

But now you'll need to show you're capable of taking on your fiercest enemy.

Channel your personal experiences to become the person you are portraying!

Remember that kid from school you really despise for bullying you and your friends in the playground?

Or that ex who dumped your sorry a** because you kiss your own entire family on the lips?

What do you mean you don't have any enemies?

What the hell is wrong with you?!

Guess that's one of the reasons you got this book hey!?

<u>IN ORDER TO CLIMB TO THE TOP YOU WILL ALWAYS ENCOUNTER ENEMIES!</u>

But as you don't have any, we'll need to revert to plan B to prepare you for your enemy poses...

"DOMINATING THE FRAME"

Locate and join your nearest **ninja school.**

Ninja's are **extremely disciplined, hugely deceptive** and capable of carrying out **incredible surprise attacks** on their enemies.

It is there you will **master** the skills required to create bad a** action poses, to take down your enemy!

CHAPTER 79

"PREP PREP PREP"

CHAPTER 79

STEP 189

"LASER FOCUSED"

Your ship has only gone and come in!

You've landed an audition for an indie movie!!...

And you didn't even have to get it off one of those dodgy websites yourself this time. You know, the ones you need to pay to subscribe to...

No, it came through your new agent!

The screenplay maybe 147 pages long, but **FOCUS** only on your potential character's lines...

NOTHING ELSE MATTERS!

AFTER ALL... CONTEXT IS FOR THOSE WHO LACK FOCUS.

The potential role of **Fan 2** is your **big opportunity**...

Hell, it's your **DEFINING MOMENT!**

It doesn't matter if you've only got one word of dialogue...

You will make that the best line of dialogue anyone has ever heard!

"PREP PREP PREP"

READ THAT DIALOGUE...
MASTER IT...
BECOME IT...
METHOD IT…

<u>LOVE THE WORDS YOU SAY AND THE WORDS YOU SAY WILL LOVE YOU BACK!</u>

CHAPTER 79

STEP 196

"HELLO AGAIN, OLD FRIEND!"

Before any audition, you need to mentally prepare.

But YOU are no longer like the others.

With this book, you now have an **advantage**...

You have the **secrets**.

YOU HAVE THE METHOD!

Remember Step 105?

It's time to **return to your ELEPHANT.**

Only this time you will no longer roam forests...

You will no longer roam the barren lands...

This time your elephant will roam the place where **Fan 2** lives...

After all...

TO BECOME THE CHARACTER, YOU FIRST NEED TO KNOW THE CHARACTER.

"PREP PREP PREP"

STEP 201

"WHERE DO I LIVE?"

You know your character's name right?

Memorized that dialogue?

You're lying on the floor?

What do you mean "no"? What are you waiting for?...

Do it now... Get on the floor. It doesn't matter where you are.

CLOSE YOUR EYES.

BREATHE...

INHALE...

EXHALE...

You are entering your place of **Zen** again.

You will slowly be transported to where **Fan 2** lives...

You are at the place of **ICONS**...

The place of **LEGENDS**...

The place where **STARS** litter the sidewalk...

CHAPTER 79

You are an **ELEPHANT** again!

Roaming the streets of Hollywood Boulevard, pounding the stars along the sidewalk, like you're awakening the acting Gods.

You're passing your adoring <u>FANS</u>, who scream your name and cheer wildly!

There are others there who have read this book

Tip your trunk to them, your method brothers and sisters.

You will notice them disguised as SUPERHEROES...

They are ahead of you on their journey. They have graduated from elephant status.

Just like you they are centering themselves...

Readying themselves for BATTLE...

Readying themselves for their AUDITION...

Readying themselves for their NEXT BIG ROLE.

<u>YOU ARE NOT ALONE.</u>

"PREP PREP PREP"

When you open your eyes you will be **ready** for your audition.

CHAPTER 83

"DARKNESS OF REJECTION"

CHAPTER 83

STEP 210

"FAILURE DOES NOT EXIST"

So you still haven't heard back from that audition?

You're thinking: *I didn't get the part...*

I probably wasn't girly enough!...

They didn't take me seriously?!...

I should have played it differently...

I should have talked to the director more...

I should have--

--ENOUGH!

THESE ARE JUST YOUR SELF-DOUBTS SPEAKING.

EMBRACE THEM.

LET THEM OUT OF YOUR SYSTEM.

THEN LICK YOUR WOUNDS.

ROME WASN'T BUILT IN A DAY.

"DARKNESS OF REJECTION"

It's time to consider the **three R's:**

REFLECT:

RE-THINK:

REJUVENATE:

~~REVENGE~~:(*SORRY THAT'S A TYPO)

#honeyourmethod

CHAPTER 83

STEP 229
"GRASS ISN'T GREENER"

Still no news from the audition?

And your agent has come up with nothing new?

Nada?...

Like zilch?!?

Jeez.

I know what you're thinking...

Maybe I need a new agent?

Maybe I'm not cut out for this?!

Maybe I need a psychologist!

OR JUST MAYBE YOU NEED TO TAKE MATTERS INTO YOUR OWN HANDS!

Breathe.

You need to calm down.

Remember Step 126... **YOU** are a **PATIENCE WARRIOR.**

"DARKNESS OF REJECTION"

CLOSE YOUR EYES...
FOCUS...

YOU MY FRIEND, WILL BE ANYONE OR ANYTHING YOU WANT TO BE.

CHAPTER 83

STEP 233

"SAME SH*T DIFFERENT DAY..."

Once in a while the sun shines down on the righteous...

And what do you know... what's that I see flickering on your phone?

You missed a call from your agent!

Righteous or not, my friend, you might have just done something good...

You just don't know it yet!

Keep the faith.

Keep on honing your method.

AND FOR GOD'S SAKE...

KEEP CALLING YOUR FREAKING AGENT BACK!

The Hollywood Gods move in mysterious ways.

CHAPTER 94

"A FALSE DAWN?"

CHAPTER 94

STEP 254

"WHERE'S MY LIFE JACKET?"

Finally heard back from your agent? All he wanted was your **updated waist measurements?!?...**

He thought you were getting *fat*!?!

Screw him!

We've all been there (Well actually I haven't, but that's by the by).

Why don't you roll another fat one up. Take your mind of everything...

Maybe this sh*t isn't working.

Maybe this is—

--STOP.

You've reached the middle of the ocean.

There's no land behind you and no land in front of you.

You are NOW ROYALLY SCREWED!

So go ahead...

Take a coin and flip for your future...

"A FALSE DAWN?"

Thought so...

Now you're thinking best of three, or best of five...

Put the coin away.

YOU ARE MEANT TO BE HERE.

When you read a book, you read it from cover to cover.

So read on my friend.

Learn.

PRACTICE... MAKES... PERFECT.

CHAPTER 94

STEP 261

"OUT WITH THE OLD"

Maybe yesterday's you was happy finishing second?

NEWSFLASH: IF YOU'RE HAPPY FINISHING SECOND, THEN ALL YOU REALLY ARE IS THE FIRST HAPPY LOSER.

Are you a loser?

Damn right you're NOT!

YOU'RE A WINNER!!

So time to **HUSTLE!**

Time to **GRIND!**

From this day forward, it's no more playing nice.

It's time to be the MOTHER F*CKING BOSS!

You will no longer smile...

You will **GROWL!**

You will no longer answer your phone with hello...

"A FALSE DAWN?"

You will answer it with **WHO CARES!**

You will no longer hold back your words...

You will say what you think!

<u>EXPRESS WHAT YOU FEEL... AND THE WORLD WILL TAKE NOTICE.</u>

CHAPTER 94

STEP 274

"SAY MY NAME!"

Would you believe it, they called you back from that audition!

I never doubted it...

You on the other hand...

Well... let's just say you're evolving and leave it at that.

Turns out you KILLED IT in your audition (not literally I hope?).

And you've made it down to the last three actors for the role!

Now it's just a waiting game right?

WRONG!

Do you really think I let you into the **SECRET OF NINJA** just for your headshots?

What do you take me for!?!

79

"A FALSE DAWN?"

Now is the time to put your secret ninja skills into practice.

It's time to be **PRO-ACTIVE**.

And it's time, my friend, to take down the competition!

Use every tool at your disposal.

NOTHING IS OFF LIMITS!

CHAPTER 109

"GOOD THINGS COME TO THOSE WHO..."

CHAPTER 109

STEP 280

"VICTORY!"

Wow, this method thing really works!

I don't know what you did, but you've only gone and landed that role!

In fact, they loved you so much they **upped you** to a **bigger part...**

FAN 1!

Congratulations!

Not sure what happened to the actor playing that role?...

Either way... Pat yourself on the back...

No for real, **DO IT NOW**...

Commend yourself for this moment. It's essential you do this.

ALWAYS BE WITH YOUR VICTORY.

YOU did this.

No one else.

"GOOD THINGS COME TO THOSE WHO..."

YOU.

YOU are 100% responsible!

AND WHEN YOU DEDICATE YOURSELF TO THE METHOD, GREAT THINGS CAN HAPPEN.

CHAPTER 109

STEP 284

"FRONT END OR BACK END"

... and no I'm not talking about your a**! Remember Step 89...

ALWAYS PROTECT YOUR A**!

I'm talking about taking care of YOU the 'BUSINESS'.

If you have been following this guide correctly you will have been making progress...

You've probably scored more auditions...

Perhaps you've landed a steady stream of roles in independent movies...

Or maybe you're now even able to pay the rent without help from daddy.

But all you see is your upfront fee from your work...

You're wondering if there is more $$$ in it for you?

Especially when some of the projects you've been involved in have made money at the box office.

"GOOD THINGS COME TO THOSE WHO..."

Well, the short answer is, of course there is!

<u>BUT, IF YOU DO NOT VALUE YOURSELF, THEN NEVER EXPECT OTHERS TO.</u>

CHAPTER 109

STEP 290

"EMERGENCY FACE TIME"

So, you're fed up making pittance $$$ to star in projects?

Want more?

Hell, **YOU** deserve more!

It's time to tell your agent how it is.

DO NOT HOLD BACK!

You **NOW** need a share of the spoils should one of your projects land and make a fortune.

You deserve it.

Without that in your deal moving forward, then you can no longer accept acting roles.

Maybe your agent thinks you're nuts.

MAYBE YOUR AGENT NEEDS HIS FAT A FIRED!!**

"GOOD THINGS COME TO THOSE WHO…"

REPEAT AFTER ME: "1% OF SOMETHING IS BETTER THAN NOTHING."

Learn this **NOW.**

Tattoo it on your forehead if you have to…

BUT NEVER EVER FORGET IT!

CHAPTER 109

STEP 293

"LAW UNTO THEMSELVES"

Despite evidence to the contrary, entertainment attorneys are human... At least, that's what I'm led to believe.

When engaging one, whatever you do, **do not under any circumstances attempt to learn their language!**

It can become confusing for the **laser focussed, method maestro** that you are...

UNLESS OF COURSE, YOU ARE PLAYING AN ACTING ROLE OF A LAWYER.

Instead, locate the best attorney in town and hire them!

It **DOESN'T MATTER** if you can't afford to pay them!...

You have the **METHOD!**

CONVINCE THEM!!

"GOOD THINGS COME TO THOSE WHO..."

The attorney who represents you is like a General leading a country into battle...

A super-smart General!

Your attorney says everything about you.

SO IF YOU WANT TO BE THE BEST, THEN HIRE THE BEST.

CHAPTER 120

"THE NEW YOU!"

CHAPTER 120

STEP 294

"DO I GET A CAPE?"

Look at you, a signed actor with a bad a** attorney... Who if you haven't already will soon be landing more and more acting gigs!

Indeed, what's that I've been reading in the latest trades?...

You've now landed a huge starring role!

Your team has even negotiated your name above the title on the poster!... And got you a big upfront fee and bad a** percentage of the 'back end' profits!

You my friend, are living out YOUR MANTRA!

YOU'VE reached SUPERHERO STATUS!

Life doesn't get much better than this.

But **remain diligent.**

Stay focused.

Keep following your method.

"THE NEW YOU!"

As beware...

SUPERHEROES ALWAYS HAVE ENEMIES.

With your success, it's inevitable you will now become a target for the **ENVY F*CKERS.**

And if you've sh*t on folks on the way up, they'll sh*t on you twice as bad on your way back down.

This is another reason you hired that expensive attorney to help protect your a**!

CHAPTER 120

STEP 297

"EMBRACE THE MISTAKES"

So now we know how your attorney can help protect you. But even he cannot guard you against the biggest danger of all...

YOUR OWN BAD A** SUPERHERO SELF!

You are living a life of method now and method my friend, is powerful.

You will make mistakes.

It's inevitable.

But whatever you do, do not be scared of making them. They will happen.

OWN THEM.

LOVE THEM.

After all, you never set out to make them.

And always remember your mistake is an opportunity...

It is an advantage, not a problem.

"THE NEW YOU!"

But even in the darkest moments where you can't believe what the f*ck you've just done, always remember your method exercises.

Breathe...

Inhale...

Exhale...

Realize a mistake for what it is…

A reminder that YOU are human…

A chance to learn quickly.

NO MATTER WHAT ALWAYS STAY TRUE TO YOUR METHOD SELF

CHAPTER 120

STEP 299

"PLAYING DETECTIVE"

Your new movie is about to be released to the world...

AND YOU MY FRIEND, ARE ABOUT TO GRADUATE TO BECOME A BIG DOG IN TOWN!

ROAR!!!

But **BEWARE** of the other **'Big Dogs'!**

They will no doubt want to be seen with you... Who wouldn't?

They'll want to become your friend...

Or maybe much more!

Sounds fun right?

YOU must **remain focussed.**

ALWAYS REMAIN ON YOUR OWN PATHWAY.

Use your ninja skills to decipher their real intentions.

"THE NEW YOU!"

Why did they mysteriously appear on your morning hike?

And how do they know you like chili dogs so much?

Why do you like chili dogs so much?

Are they method acting just to get close to you?

BEWARE THEIR INTENTIONS MAY NOT BE GENUINE!

CHAPTER 144

"WORLD FAMOUS!"

CHAPTER 144

STEP 300

"NO LIMITS"

You've done it!

You've struck **GOLD!**

YOUR MOVIE HAS JUST BEEN RELEASED AND HAS ONLY GONE AND SMASHED IT AT THE BOX OFFICE!

I don't know how you ended up landing that role?

Was it anything to do with those photos you took of the director doing "that thing" with the guy from that place?

Don't answer that.

Either way...

Congratulations BIG DOG you've finally ARRIVED!

But your work does not stop there.

NOW YOUR CHALLENGE IS ABOUT STAYING AT THE TOP!

"WORLD FAMOUS!"

AND SOON, BIG DOG, IT WILL BE ABOUT YOU CREATING THE NEW TOP!

<u>AFTER ALL, THE LIMITS OF WHAT YOU CAN ACHIEVE, ARE ONLY SET BY YOURSELF.</u>

CHAPTER 144

STEP 311

"FIESTA FOREVER"

Now you're a **bona fide star,** the awards season is no longer a big fat waste of time.

Especially because YOU may well actually get nominated!

Unbelievable isn't it...

A bit like the time when you went to get that tattoo done on your... Yeah, we probably shouldn't go into that again.

Opportunities aplenty are going to fall your way to party and network with Hollywood royalty!

Decide which of your genuine Big Dog friends you will run with.

PLAN WHERE YOU WILL BE SEEN WITH PRECISION!

BEING SPOTTED AT THE WRONG PLACE AT THE WRONG TIME IS CAREER SUICIDE!

And you only just arrived here, so don't screw it up now!

This is temptation season. Beware the dangers that come with it.

You must **REMAIN VIGIL.**

YOU MUST ALWAYS REMAIN IN CHARACTER, AS THE PERSON YOU ARE AND THE PERSON YOU WANT TO BE...

<u>YESTERDAY'S YOU IS LURKING JUST OVER YOUR SHOULDER.</u>

CHAPTER 144

STEP 325

"I'D LIKE TO THANK..."

So you only went and got you're a** nominated for that award!

You deserve it!

Now, you will have a chance to talk on stage in front of your peers, as well as a live TV audience of millions. A nerve-racking moment for some...

BUT NOT FOR THIS BIG DOG!

You my friend, are **dressed for success** today. You will rock that stage with grace, like the Big Dog you've become.

Finally, you will hear the **true power of your name** when it's announced by the presenter.

In your **victory speech** you will no doubt want to thank all those that have made you the actor you are today.

But a word of caution...

NEVER GET CARRIED AWAY IN THE MOMENT.

This is perhaps the most valuable opportunity you have to showcase your method skills.

Crying wouldn't go amiss, but I'd probably avoid any ninja poses, they might send off the wrong message.

IT'S TIME TO SHOW THE WORLD THE POWER OF YOUR VOICE.

This is your moment to attract a whole new legion of fans, who will instantly fall in love with you if you play this moment right.

CHAPTER 155

"CROSSROADS"

CHAPTER 155

STEP 333

"GROWING STALE?"

So it's been months since you won that award, so I got to ask, why on *earth* are you still sleeping with it?!

You're feeling like you could accomplish more aren't you?

Growing tired of the adulation of your adoring fans?... Who probably only love you for being in "that" now award-winning movie anyway... Or for crying on stage during your acceptance speech!

You may have acted in many projects since, all of them striking box office gold. But all your fans want to talk to you about is "that" same freaking movie.

Maybe you'll always just play the funny role and could never do the bad a** gangster role?

STOP!

Breathe.

Remember...

YOU WERE ONCE AN ELEPHANT!

NEVER EVER FORGET WHERE YOU'VE COME FROM.

"CROSSROADS"

Close your eyes.

Focus.

Remember your method...

"I WILL BE ANYONE OR ANYTHING I WANT TO BE..."

That's it.

Inhale...

Exhale...

<u>REINVENTION IS ONLY THE BATTLE WITH ONESELF.</u>

Look for that bigger mountain. Do you see it?

YOU will climb it.

YOU will conquer it.

YOU will stand triumphant atop it!

The world will hear YOU roar again!

CHAPTER 155

STEP 337

"ANOTHER SIDE OF YOU!"

So you persuaded your agent of your new career direction? Wow, how the hell did you pull that off?...

Actually, don't answer that.

And now you've landed an audition for that bad a** gangster role you crave so bad!...

That no one in their right mind would ever cast you for!!...

Bravo.

...Only to discover, there's been a MISTAKE and the director ACTUALLY wants to hire you in the FUNNY ROLE you always play!

Screw that director!

Or maybe it was your agent's doing? Probably terrified that you are about to blow up your whole entire career?!

You're frustrated. Annoyed.

They don't think you're capable.

YOU KNOW YOU'RE CAPABLE!

"CROSSROADS"

Maybe this isn't the first time this has happened.

Maybe it won't be the last.

You're ready to snap!

Breathe.

Always remain in control of your emotions!

THOSE WHO CAN STEP OUT OF THEMSELVES AT TIMES LIKE THESE, WILL FIND THE SOLUTION.

CHAPTER 155

STEP 356

"IT'S NOT OVERNIGHT"

'No one in their right mind would ever cast you in that role'!...

...Those fateful words are still ringing in your ears, right?

STOP!

YOU DON'T KNOW IT NOW, BUT THESE WORDS ARE THE BEST DAMN THING ANYONE HAS EVER SAID ABOUT YOU.

No, I'm not crazy!... And no, I haven't been smoking anything!

Use these words to your advantage...

Let them fuel your inner fire.

YOU WERE ONCE AN ELEPHANT...

THEN A SUPERHERO...

NOW, MY FRIEND, YOU'RE THE F*CKING BIG DOG!

YOU CAN DO ANYTHING.

"CROSSROADS"

YOU'VE SHOWN THAT.

YOU HAVE THE METHOD...

NOW IT'S TIME FOR YOU TO EVOLVE AGAIN!

<u>YOU WILL BE ANYONE OR ANYTHING YOU WANT TO BE!</u>

CHAPTER 169

"PASSING ON THE MESSAGE"

CHAPTER 169

STEP 377

"THE FINAL STEP"

When you look in the mirror now, what do you see?

Look closer...

Real close.

I'll tell you what you see.

You see **TODAY**...

You see **TOMORROW**...

YOU SEE SUCCESS!

It's time to share the message...

BUT NOT JUST TO ANYONE.

This book should only be shared with those YOU deem worthy...

Those who would appreciate it for what it is...

Those who are ready for the secrets within...

Those who truly want to prosper and advance in life.

"PASSING ON THE MESSAGE"

IF YOU CHOOSE TO SHARE THIS BOOK, CHOOSE IT'S NEXT KEEPER WISELY.

MAKE SURE THEY ARE READY TO LEARN THE STEPS OF THE METHOD.

ABOUT THE AUTHOR

Not a lot is known about Rob Weston, except the obvious, that he invented writing and acting, and of course, was the first person to swim the Atlantic Ocean utilizing just doggy paddle.

Some say that Rob lives a quiet life with the monks, deep in the mountains of South Korea, others swear they saw him, teaching 'method', while straddling the Hollywood Sign. Wherever he is, whatever he is doing, one thing is for certain… Rob doesn't just write self-help guides, he also writes fiction.

Visit us at:
WWW.MOVIESTARRATING.COM

Made in the USA
Coppell, TX
03 December 2022

87760262R00090